Glimpses

Of

God's Faithfulness

By

Dede Dorsey Toney

Xulon
PRESS

Glimpses Of God's Faithfulness
by Dede Dorsey Toney

Printed in the United States of America

ISBN 1-594676-66-6

Unless otherwise indicated, Bible quotations are taken from the New American Standard Version. Copyright © 1979 by Moody Press.

Written by Dede Dorsey Toney
Edited by Barbara Fox
Book Design by Xulon Press

www.xulonpress.com

Contents

Special Thanks

Special thanks to my husband Robert T. Toney Sr. whose love and encouragement over these past twenty-one years have given me the freedom to be used by God. Thanks, honey, for listening to all my dreams and for being a vital part of making the publishing of this book a reality.

Hearty acknowledgements are made to my four children, Melissa, Michelle, Melinda and Robert Jr. To my parents, Fred and Margaret Dorsey Sr., and to my brothers and sisters, Freda Ayers, Pamela Nash, Paula Wilkinson, Jennifer Dorsey, Fred Dorsey Jr., Jeffery Dorsey, Maretta Dorsey, Zanetta Dorsey and Christopher Dorsey. I also would like to thank a host of friends and relatives, who have loved, supported and encouraged me throughout the years to "walk with the Lord."

Dedication

*T*his book is dedicated to my husband Robert T. Toney Sr. who has encouraged me to be the wife and mom God has called me to be.

Thank you Rob, for your love and sacrifices that have resulted in the publishing of my first book.

I love you!

Foreword Introductions

My foreword will be written by three Godly men who have had a major impact on my life: My father Fred M. Dorsey Sr., my pastor Dr. Anthony T. Evans and my assistant pastor Dr. Martin E. Hawkins.

My father is a great Godly influence in my life. As a little girl growing up, he modeled to me the value of family. He let me see a precious treasure, integrity. He taught the value of character and modeled that character as well. He showed me who was important in his life which gave me a desire to want Christ for myself. Dad, thanks for having such high expectations for me and for modeling to me Christlikeness. Because of your love for me, I learned to love and trust a God I could not see.

Dr. Anthony T. Evans is the Senior pastor of Oak Cliff Bible Fellowship church in Dallas, Texas. I came to visit the church in March of 1981 when he preached the sermon, "What is that in your hand?" He shared that, with Christ as Lord and Savior, our lives are victorious and no matter what we have done or what trials we face, Christ already paid it all with his death and resurrection. Dr. Evans was the instrument that God used for me to give my life to Christ. That day he shared that there is no life without Christ. We are empty, only existing, but with Christ, we can do all things. Dr. Evans, thank you for letting God use your life. As a result of your obedience to preach the Word, I now have a personal relationship with Christ as my Lord and Savior.

Dr. Martin E. Hawkins is the assistant pastor of Oak Cliff Bible Fellowship. He was extremely instrumental in helping me grow in

Christ. He was my father away from home who mentored me as I grew and developed spiritually. He taught me by example the joys of walking with the Lord. Dr. Hawkins, thank you for living a life before me where I was able to actively see Christ. Thanks for the many ways you encouraged me to always seek Christ.

Foreword By Fred M. Dorsey, Sr.

Fred and Margaret Dorsey are proud parents of Dede, the oldest of seven girls and three boys. She is the great dreamer of our family-bubbly, full of joy and grace with a huge smile. In the only world she knows, her life is filled with children and adults of every age. Therefore, she seems to be undoubtedly committed to being the channel of hope for God's promises to children who learn differently and to people of all ages who may benefit from her God-given gifts and talents. The true spirit of God's love in Dede is buried deeply in the recesses of her consciousness. It is expressed in her character, poems, plays, and teaching, which gives evidence to the major storehouse of gifts from which she extracts the talents. She uses these gifts to transfer God's blessings to those whose lives she touches to make them anew.

Dede's great capacity to achieve, as may be measured by man, is not extraordinary, but the capacity of her heart and her passion to do miraculous and extraordinary things for those damaged by life, and those uniquely special, is impeccable. I believe the kind of extraordinary person she is, has prepared her to do extraordinary things for others through God's special guidance and help. It is, therefore, this very unique feather and gift from God that she has provided *Glimpses of God's Faithfulness,* not for personal use, but as a hope to keep others encouraged.

Foreword By Dr. Anthony T. Evans

Mrs. Dede Toney is one of the finest Christian women I know. Dede has been graced by the Creator with a blend of qualities, character, and gifts that places her in the category of a modern-day Wonderwoman.

A wife and mother, she would be an excellent poster girl for the woman of Proverbs 31. Not merely because she takes good care of her family, but also because that care emanates from a heart that fears God.

Dede is also known for her servant heart. As her pastor, I am keenly aware of her willingness to give generously of her time to serve others and allow the joy of her heart to bring joy to the hearts of those who need it. Such selflessness today is hard to find.

Dede is also uniquely gifted when it comes to writing poetry. She can take any situation, any event, or any person and create a sonnet that not only fits the topic but also inspires the listener. Many an event, of which I have been a part, have been illuminated by poetic genius of Dede's voice reading one of her poems with dignity and grace.

Dede is one of those once in a life time ladies. To meet her is to be inspired by her mere presence. To hear her is to be challenged by her incredibly powerful ideas, and to know her is to be transformed by her impeccable character.

Dede Toney is the personification of all God had in mind when He created a woman.

Foreword By Martin E. Hawkins

There aren't many who can mix skills that are equally gifted in multiple areas, and yet use them for the good of others. Dede Toney is one of those who can. She has the elegance to read, write and recite poetry while still being an exemplary mother of four.

Her abilities also extend to athletic activities where she participates and encourages her children to strive for the highest form of excellence in their field of endeavors. Those same motherly touches are seen in her ability to walk beside each child to know well, his/her weaknesses and strengths.

Blending these talents, gifts, skills and or abilities causes Dede to relate to others who have varied backgrounds. Each of her writings is uniquely crafted and they form a collage of her experiences that makes all she writes a tender loving approach to life.

Preface

You may ask, "Who are you? I have never seen or heard about you. What do you have to tell us that we have not heard already?" Well, to answer your possible questions, I am an ordinary person who is a wife and mother of three teenagers and a twenty-year-old. I am a first grade teacher of fourteen years as well as a Certified Academic Language Therapist. I have no Grammies, no Oscars, no footprints in Hollywood, and no nominations into the Hall of Fame. All I know is that God uses ordinary people who are willing to use their gifts for His Glory. I was willing. Have you ever dreamed of doing something so badly but did not have enough courage and belief in yourself to pursue it? That describes me. I had a passion to write and I lived in the bookstores just gazing at many different kinds of books. Many times I said, " I know I can write about that," or "Man! That is the way I feel, too." It seemed these people were writing what I felt. I often went to the Lord and asked for His assistance, and His response was, "I have given it to you. JUST DO IT!" And everytime I began to believe in myself, doubt would set in. My question then became, "Who would want to listen to me?" Satan would answer back so loudly, "NOBODY!" And I began to believe it. I am glad God keeps encouraging us through His word and through friends. The verse that I adopted and held dear to my heart was Jeremiah 33:3: "Call to me and I will answer you, and I will tell you great and mighty things, which you do not know." I wanted that promise so I kept calling and inching my way, writing one letter at a time. With much encouragement from my husband Robert Sr., my children, my parents, sisters, brothers, aunts, uncles, cousins, friends and church family, this book was born.

Who will listen to me? Those who God sends. I am thankful to all of you who have invested in my life. This is definitely a dream come true.

Introduction

As a little girl, I traveled with my family, to see our grandparents in the summer. I was always fascinated that the sun followed us from state to state. I asked my dad if every state had its own sun, and if not, how could the sun follow us everywhere we went? After a long pause, he finally answered. His response was that the sun does not move. We move. And sometimes, when we do not see it, it does not mean it is not there. When I came to accept the Lord in 1981, I applied that same principle. The Son is always present even when our lives are cloudy. I am so glad that there is nowhere on earth we can go that He is not there. So if you are traveling down a lonely road in life or experiencing the struggles of life, please know and be encouraged that the "Son is able to do exceedingly abundantly beyond all that we ask or think according to the power that works within us." (Ephesians 3:2). Try Him, you will not be disappointed.

This book contains glimpses of God's faithfulness in my life. He was faithful before I accepted Him, and He continues to show His faithfulness. As you will see in each chapter, the Lord was growing me spiritually through my writing. I do not know how He does it, but I am grateful. I do know however, that He patiently waits until we get the message or the lessons He wants us to learn. My prayer is that the words on these pages will be lifted off the page into your hearts and become words that will keep you encouraged. I pray that you will gain strength as you continue your journey with Christ.

Young and Restless

*B*eing the oldest of ten children, I often found myself the center of my brothers' and sisters' watchful eyes. Somehow they bought into my Mom's and dad's theory that their big sister was a good example. Believe me, they kept me on my toes. My first writing experience came out of a not-so-good experience. I was a teenager lost in myself, and I wrote my first poem at that time of my life. I was experiencing pressure from school and home and did not quite know how to express myself. I was young and restless with myself and with life. I felt like I knew much about life, but according to my parents, I had only begun to live, and if I wanted all the benefits of home, I had to make sure I followed their rules and managed my life within their rules. You know, as a teenager, we think we know more than our parents do. Life somehow becomes big and nothing seems important but us. The emotions are off the charts, and with me, I did not have an older sister or brother to talk to and so I felt stuck. Writing was my only outlet. I began to write all the time and little did I know that God was working in my life even though I did not know Him as Lord and Savior. He wove into me the passion to write. Sometimes when I was writing, I was so amazed at the outcome. I would start writing, not even thinking about what I was writing and when it was completed, I could not believe it. Each letter formed words that lifted off the page when I read it back to myself. It was as if God were letting me know He had been listening to me all along and telling me He would never leave me. His love would be a forever imprint within my heart. That is the reason I named my book *Glimpses of God's Faithfulness.* As you read through this book, you will see how God grew me, one word at a time.

If you are a teenager, remember there are many positive things you can do through this stage. I found that when I focused on others, my situation was not as bad as it seemed. Let me say that disrespecting and disobeying your parents is not the way to go. It only prolongs God's blessings in your life and it causes relational division. "Children obey your parents in the Lord for this is right. Honor your Father and Mother that it may be well with you" (Ephesians 6:1-3). Believe me, YOU WILL need your parents in your life, and you do not want to ruin that relationship just because you are going through the teenage years. There will be many more stages in your life that will be tougher that this one. I do not know if you know the Lord, but He is your only source of strength as you walk through this phase of life. Trust Him; travel with Him. He makes a dependable companion. The remarkable thing about Him is that He will not let you down and He is a person of His word.

Now, if you are a parent of a teenager, the best thing you can do is STAND. Do not throw away your standards because your child throws a tantrum or refuses to talk to you. Those are just emotions coming out. Be loving, but firm. Keep telling your teenager how valuable he is to you. Bring out the best in him because the world and this stage are bringing out the worst. For no reason, treat him to his favorite place. Or write him a letter. What I am saying is that teenagers need you to remain parents. You are the only stable force in their world. So be encouraged that this stage will pass, but you are needed in the process. Above all else, stay on your knees before the Lord and ask Him, as my parents did, how to raise this precious child He has given you. He is the best counselor for the job and His way is always right!

Young And Restless

Being a teenager is stressful for goodness sakes
And to top it all off I have bumps on my face.
My body won't fit in any of my clothes,
But I must act cool so no one knows.
That I feel lost and lonely every day
And I try to act cool in a not-so-cool way,
Things that I know that are right to do
I sacrifice them so I can be cool.
I'm a teenager now with so much to know.
Lord order my steps as I grow.
Each day I'm in school I try to act tough,
But I'm finding that being tough isn't enough.
I need inner acceptance about myself
And I need encouragement if nothing else
To stand among my friends in sight
And do the things I know are right.
So God I need you everyday
Letting me know that I'm ok.
Can You give me courage through all my fears,
so I can get through these teenage years?

© Dede Toney

Eternally Secured

Many years have passed since I was a teenager, but what I have found is that wanting to be accepted is not restricted by age, gender, status or race; everyone wants to know how he fits in. He needs to know that there is something good about him.

When I went off to college, I wanted so badly to fit in. I was certainly different. Many of the girls had experienced so much of life that I did not know. They looked grown up and I was still looking like a little kid. I saw girls with clothes on that my mother forbade me to wear. I tried to wear them, but something inside of me did not let me feel comfortable. In college I also experienced religion pressures. I know my parents taught me well, but what I realized in college was that I had to make decisions about my life. I had to believe because I knew, not just because they told me. For the first time, I felt like I was on a life search. Many things that once were secure for me were now becoming shaky. What I thought I believed and understood, I now questioned. I was confused and had so many questions I needed answered.

I was engaged to be married in August of 1981, and I was trying to plan a trip to Dallas to find a job in teaching. I did not have the funds or the time off from my part time job. I did not know where the funds were coming from or how I was going to get the time off, but Spring break was coming up and I needed a break. To make a long story short, God set things in motion, and I was on my way to Dallas, Texas. When I boarded the plane, I was very nervous. I sat by the window and tried to calm myself. A gentleman sat beside me with his work papers in hand and when the plane reached a safe altitude and the seatbelt sign was turned off, he went right to work. He did not appear worried about the flight at all. He took one look at me and asked if I were all right. I told him "no" and we began to chat. In our conversation he said, "Whether you fly or drive a car, you should not let fear spoil your fun. If you are in Christ, you are eternally secured, and if the plane crashes or the car wrecks, you will be with the Lord. So relax. Go to sleep. You will be in Dallas in no time." As I closed my eyes, I peeked at this guy amazed because he spoke with such confidence and security. I drifted off to sleep and before I knew it, I was in Dallas. My fear disappeared when I met my fiancé at the gate.

After spending almost a week in Dallas, I ended my trip attending Oak Cliff Bible Fellowship, a church my husband had been writing me about. Dr .Anthony Evans is the pastor. That Sunday his opening line was, "What is keeping you from asking Christ to be the Lord of your life?" That day, as I sat in church, it was as if I were the only one there. Everything he said from then on was as if he were talking to me. He said, "No one can give you a personal relationship with Christ but you. You must do that for yourself. You cannot continue to live on your parents' relationship. You have to commit to the Lord yourself." He continued to share that God saw us in a hopeless state on our way to hell. He knew we could never enjoy fellowship with Him if we stayed in our sinful state. What really got my attention was when Pastor Evans said, "It is Christ and Christ alone that gives us eternal life. No works, no goodness can do it. Without Him we only exist." He tied it to the story of Moses. The staff Moses had was lifeless. It was useless. It was just a staff. But when Moses released it, God did above and beyond all Moses could imagine. Moses had to let it go and let God be God. I am sure I have heard similar words from my parents and others, but on this particular day, my eyes were opened to the truth. I had been struggling spiritually, and it seemed the more I worked on it, the more confusing it became. I needed someone to sort through my mess, clean me up, start me over and encourage me everyday. At the end of his sermon he asked if anyone wanted to make a decision to give his life over to Christ and let Him be Lord and Savior. He said, "Christ is able to guide you and lead you. You do not have to keep trying to do it on your own. He wants to save you from hopelessness and spiritual death, death that would eternally separate you from Him forever. He can take away all your sins and give you the power to live for Him." I needed and wanted that in my life, but I did not know I did not have to work for it, or be good to receive it, or try to change everything on my own. Knowing Christ could do all of that for a lonely, shy, young lady like me was overwhelming. I sat there and asked Christ to be my Lord and Savior. I did not know what all that meant, but I was willing to give Christ a try. God planned that trip, and He was waiting there for me. He used Pastor Evans' sermon to bring me into His saving knowledge so I could have power to live for Him.

So if you are hesitant about accepting Christ in your life, do not be. If you are trying to change to meet Him, do not. If you feel you are beyond His acceptance, do not. Christ died just for you. He does not want you to fix yourself. He wants that honor. He wants to fellowship with you. No fixing in the world would help a life without Christ. Pastor Evans shared the gospel. The Lord had been preparing me since I was young to meet Him in this way. He filled me up with the good news of Jesus Christ. As a result of my acceptance of the gospel, my spiritual heart pump was turned ON! When I boarded the plane at the end of the week, I wrote the Lord a letter expressing to Him how grateful I was that He waited for me. I called it "Eternally Secured."

I pray that you will come to know Christ as Lord and Savior. That is His plan. He will not force you. He will not beg you. He will patiently wait, but once you have heard the gospel, do not allow yourself to put off making the decision. He loves you so much that He gave his very life for you. Let Him free you and eternally secure you. Let Him be your Lord and Savior. I promise, you will not ever regret it!

Eternally Secured

Lord help me as a new Christian to be committed to live for You
May I thirst for Your will in life, as to what I need to do.
Help me to make right choices, when I'm tempted throughout the day,
So that through my life of living for You,
I'll bring my friends Your way.

May I always be an example, a leader and a friend,
So as I grow in You, dear Lord, many souls to You I'll win.
Thank you, Lord, for waiting and seeking after me
because now I can say, I'm truly Your child, with eternal security.
©Dede Toney

My Daily Bread

$\mathcal{A}$s a young child growing up, we always said "The Lord's Prayer." There was one part in there that came to life before my very eyes, and that was "Give us this day our daily bread."(Matt 6:11). Mom explained it as having the Lord provide what ever we needed each day. Well, one day my mom cooked supper for the family. There was always enough to go around, but not for guests unless Mama planned it. This one particular day Mom had just finished cooking dinner, and we were ready to assemble together at the table. (By the way, my parents did not permit individual eating. We ate full course meals together at least five times a week.) The doorbell rang and it was some friends we had not seen for a while. They had been traveling and just decided to stop by and say hello. The first thing my mom did was offer them some food. I remember so clearly asking myself, "How can she do that?" We only have enough for the family." My Mom never hesitated. She made the guests feel comfortable and went into the kitchen and made all four of them a plate. She then proceeded to fix our plates. We added the section to the table, and we all ate together. I was speechless. How could that have happened? I knew Mom did not prepare enough. I was there helping her cook that day. I believe God multiplied the food. How He did it I cannot begin to tell you, but I admired my mom so much more that day because she trusted God to meet the needs, seen and unseen.

So the next time people stop by and you know you have not prepared enough and you genuinely want to feed them, trust God for the seen and the unseen and JUST SERVE!

This food my Mom cooked nourished my physical body. When I came to know the Lord, my spiritual body was hungry for His word. I wanted to catch up on all that I had missed. I knew if physical food was important, surely, spiritual food was even more important. Months passed and I graduated from college, got married and moved to Dallas all in the same year. Fortunately, God surrounded me with people who were on fire for Him. That was when Dr. Martin Hawkins came into my life. He was a wise man and very personal. Even though he had many things to do, he took time to talk to me and answer any questions I had. He showed me that no matter how big we are, we must learn to serve others. When he talked about Christ being a servant, it was easy for me to understand because I saw that same trait in my parents and my husband, and I was now seeing it through him as well. He stretched me beyond what I thought I could do. He gave me good advice and wise counsel. He stressed to me, that in order to know Christ, I had to read his Word daily and apply it to every area of my life. I had to choose to live for Christ. I could not try to buy Christ by trying to be good or doing right. I had to accept the fact that I was a sinner and remind myself I had power to say no to it. The power came when I read the Word and hid the words in my heart. It came when I applied it to life's situations. I was not faithful all the time; I stumbled often, but I certainly knew from the times that I did apply God's Word, it worked. I dove into the Word and from it I wrote a poem entitled "My Daily Bread."

Do not panic if you are not doing what God asks of you. Just allow yourself a new start everyday; He does. His mercies are new and fresh everyday. I had to learn to forgive myself and move on. Remember, it was His love that drew you and it will be your love for Him that will keep you drawn. He will not leave you or forsake you even when your love is not present. I promise. He is faithful, and His Word is life!

My Daily Bread

Master, I give You my life everyday.
You are the greatest in everyway.

Daily You teach me and love me too, and You
Always know just what to do.
In good and bad times You are always there
Letting me know that You really care
You are my life and I want only You.

Be with me Lord in all that I do.
Right my heart to do Your will.
Even in hard times help me be still.
And when I'm sad or feeling blue,
Don't let me seek anyone but You!

©Dede Toney

The Wedding Talk

How many of you remember the planning of your wedding? Was it a stressful time? It was for me. The hardest part was trying to please everyone or not to leave anyone out. The night before my wedding I was sad, not because I was getting married, but because I was leaving such a wonderful family behind. My sisters and brothers were still young, and I was about to miss out on most of their lives. I also struggled with separating from my parents. My mom sensed something was wrong and she knew just what words to say. She told me that she and my dad loved me and would be thinking about me and praying for me. She told me that they were so proud of all I had accomplished thus far in my life. She continued by saying she and Dad were sad to see me go and that it was difficult for them to let me go, but they knew, in order for me to be one with my husband, I needed their support. She encouraged me to depend on the Lord and seek His guidance for my marriage. She knew her love for me was great, but God's love was greater. She encouraged me to continue my time with the Lord because she knew the value of putting Him first. Her final challenge to me was to be a woman that pleased God. That, my friends, was the most valuable wedding present I could have received. Those words stuck with me, and whenever struggles come my way, that challenge is what I remember.

If you are a parent and find it hard to let go, trust God to take care of your son or daughter. Believe me, no one can do it like He can. Parents, your words to that son or daughter before his or her wedding day will provide fuel for the marriage race. When you see

them getting weak, keep bathing them with prayer and encouragement. They need your support.

I wrote a poem that night thanking my mom for her wedding
talk.

The Wedding Talk

Thank you, Lord, for a mom so wise
Who knew what was pleasing in Your eyes.
Thank you, Mom, for our woman-to-woman talk
For reminding me to seek God in my marriage walk.
Your talk calmed my heart and gave me much rest
So that I could face my wedding day with great happiness.
Mom, thanks for the love you have for me
And for being a role model for me to see.
Thank you for the challenge that you gave me
To please the Lord and walk faithfully.

©Dede Toney

A Saving Walk

Months had now passed since I got married, ten months to be exact, and we were expecting our first child in a month. In the meantime, our church had planned a citywide evangelistic crusade through the neighborhood. Now, I knew Christ as Lord and Savior, but I had never witnessed to anyone before, so this was quite an experience. I went out with a good friend named Van Howard who showed me what to do. I watched him quite closely trying to make sure I had the words down. Do you have the words down? Are they in your heart? If so, you must share them. This kind of news is worth telling and little did I know just how God was going to use this experience. It was May of 1982 when I received a phone call from Robert's sister telling me that their mom was diagnosed with cancer and given only two months to live. When Rob heard the news, it really tested his faith. He knew God did not make mistakes, but "Why?" he kept asking himself. His mom was all he had. She wanted grandkids, and he wanted her to experience that. Rob went to Huntsville, Alabama to help take care of her. I stayed here in Dallas getting ready for our baby. His mom wanted a granddaughter, and she would say, "I am praying that for me." I myself wanted a son; in fact, a girl had not entered my prayer request. but in her mind, I was having a girl. This was a trying month. Have you ever had days or months when you just wanted to die because the pain of your situation hurt so badly? I could only imagine Rob's pain. I had not experienced a life-threatening situation with a parent so the only thing I could do was pray and be an ear for him. The pain in his life was so great during this time that he did not want to hear about the fact that

God understood and that He would walk with Him, but I thank God that no matter the grief, no matter the pain, His presence is able to take us through anything. I mean anything. You may not be experiencing the possible death of a loved one; it may be something else. Just know that He understands how you feel and just what you need to bring you through. Trust His presence.

The baby was a girl, and we named her Melissa. She was the first grandchild in both families, and it was a happy time although we faced a heartbreaking situation. Melissa was born two weeks early which gave us a chance to go and see Rob's mom. She was, indeed, very sick. Rob was scheduled to take high school kids to a Young Life Camp, and I encouraged him to go on the trip while I took care of his mom. His mom and I had a great time. She was happy to see Melissa and to spend time with her. On the other hand, I remembered Rob telling me that his mom did not know Christ. He had always wanted that for her, but it just did not happen. All I knew was that somehow I had to share Christ with her. Every night I asked God to give me just the right time and the boldness to share as well. I was there several weeks, and during the last week of my stay, I was washing dishes when his mom called me into her bedroom. She was watching TBN, and they were talking about going to heaven. She did not quite understand what they were saying, and she wanted me to explain. What an opportunity! What timing! God knew exactly how to get the process started. I answered her questions, and that night she prayed the sinner's prayer and accepted Christ as Lord and Savior. What a privilege; what joy! Words could not explain how I felt. God had trained me with my walk through the neighborhood. All that I had heard and studied was just His way of getting me ready to do His will, and that was to share His word about His Son Jesus. He wanted Rob's mom in heaven with Him more than Rob did, and he was just waiting for the timing. It was perfect. We left in July, and in September she died. What a great testimony to the power of God's Word. That walk through the neighborhood was what God used to win a soul.

I do not know if you know Christ, but if you do, share Him; a life depends on it. It is a matter of life or death, heaven or hell. I was never the same that day after I realized what had happened. Just think, the God of the universe loved us so much that He gave us His only son Jesus who dwelt among us. He walked to Calvary, carrying a cross on his back so that others would know how much He loved them. If He could walk knowing he was going to die, surely we can walk the neighborhoods telling others how to live. My friend, do not let time find you not sharing life's news,

J-E-S-U-S.

A Saving Walk

Lord, Thank you for my neighborhood walk,
that helped me to share Your life-saving talk.
Thank you, Lord, for using me,
to share Your word so others can see
that You are the way and You are the life.
You were the ultimate sacrifice.
Your love kept you hanging on a tree
So all could live eternally.

©Dede Toney

"It's..."

*A*fter the birth of our first daughter and the death of my husband's mom, life began slowly to get back to normal. Fifteen months had passed, and I was about to deliver again. I had taken the Lamaze class with my first child and so I was convinced I could remember how to breathe. I told my husband that we did not need a refresher course. That was a serious mistake. I had forgotten how to breathe, and I refused to wait to dilate. The pain was great, and I wanted medicine. I wanted an epidural, but the doctor had warned me that if I had it, it would slow down my contractions. I did not care. I wanted relief! I convinced the doctor to give me the numbing medication.

Are not our lives like that? We try to live on past blessings and we stop walking and trusting. God's desire for us is to continue to practice his teaching even if there is no pain. Being confident of knowing the steps is not the same as practicing them.

Think about it, if we just read God's Word and know It inside out but never put it into practice, its effect will never be known.. We will only know the procedure and will never experience His Power. Believe me, the storms of life is not when you want to try to find out if God is faithful. You need to know before that time. What am I saying? I am saying I should have been practicing the Lamaze technique during the times before labor, when I did not need it. Instead, I had to try to remember as I was going through the pain. God wants us to practice walking while life does not hurt. So when the storms come, and they will come, we will be ready. The labor with my second child was long. I was not in any more pain, but I was uncomfortable. Sometimes life is only uncomfortable and blessings are delayed when we stop walking and practicing. I finally delivered and the baby was another girl. We named her Michelle. She was precious and a breath of fresh air as well as a playmate for Melissa. I realized after looking at her, all the pain was worth it. That must have been how Christ felt. He loved us so much that when He thought of the pain, He said, "You are worth it."

My friend, you are worth it. No matter what cards life has dealt you, just know you have a Master dealer who holds the future, and because He holds it, it is His business to give you all that you need to accomplish His purpose. Know He can sustain your life, too. A new life came into our family; it was a girl. A new life can come into your life as well, a personal relationship with Christ. So instead of asking **what** is it, ask **who** is He? He is Jesus, the life-giver. Try Him. You will like Him! This next poem speaks of just that.

"It's..."

When life is confusing and it hurts really bad,
Jesus will give you what you've never had.
Love that reaches to your deepest pain
Even when you're empty His love remains.
Who is He? one might ask.
He's the Alpha and Omega
The beginning and the last
He's the Promised one of old
Who is more precious than any gold.
So keep reading and keep growing
cause when life's pain hit,
His name is worth knowing.

©Dede Toney

A Miracle

With two little girls and a husband in youth ministry, my life was far from boring. Melissa, almost four, and Michelle, turning two in three weeks, kept me on the go, and I was expecting our third child. I WANTED A BOY! This was my only prayer. This time, when it was time for labor, I was ready. We arrived at the hospital, and I patiently waited for the doctor. He came and told me I was having false labor so he sent me home. This false labor thing happened twice during the next two weeks. While we were waiting, I decided to give Michelle a birthday party because the baby was soon to be born, and I did not want to short-change her special day. When I got up that morning to get ready for the party, my water broke. I knew the labor was real this time. Rob and I went to the hospital, and they admitted me and gave me my epidural. Labor was progressing right along until the nurses came in the room to check me. They did not say anything, but they just went out and brought in two more nurses and a doctor. They informed us the baby's heart rate was dropping, and they might have to do an emergency c-section. I started crying. Rob was really trying to console me, and what did he use? Scripture. At that moment, I knew how he felt when I gave him scriptures when His mom was dying. I did not need scripture or a sermon. I needed God to show up. I needed a miracle. I wanted my baby to be all right, and I could only cry. I had no words to say to God, but I knew He knew what was happening. I knew He was able; I just wanted Him to do it for me. I knew I had to settle myself, accept whatever was about to happen, and trust Him to take care of me; so much easier said than done. I did not know what He was showing me, but I wanted to learn it that instant so that everything could be better.

Is that not the way we operate with God sometimes? We only call God when trouble arises. Then we want to rush His decision and move on, not owning up to our disobedience or our selfishness. What I have found is that God is still faithful. He is moving even when we cannot see Him. Another thing we sometimes do is quote all the scriptures we know back to Him as if that will help Him act faster or in our favor. Whatever the situation, God knows how we feel and what we need. I still continued to cry with no words to interpret, but boy, I am glad God knows how we feel. Just as they prepared me for the C-section, my baby's heart rate went back to normal and I was able to deliver normally. It was another girl and we named her Melinda. She was beautiful and definitely a miracle. Later on, I realized what God was trying to tell me. The problem was that during the whole time I was pregnant, I prayed more for a boy than for a baby that was healthy. He knew what I wanted and He knew what He was going to give me. His Word says to ask, but to ask according to His will. I am learning that God's will always has a purpose, and it is always Kingdom oriented.

So the next time you pray, be specific and then let God's will be done. Give Him permission to do His will in your life. This next poem is entitled "The Miracle." Incidentally, she was born on her sister's birthday.

"A Miracle"

She is a miracle with fingers and toes,
Two eyes, two ears, and a nose.
All parts of her body are functioning strong
And Lord, you were with me all along.
You never stopped caring or loving me
Even when I was selfish and too blind to see
That my daughter's heart belonged to you
And that You were able to bring her through.
Thank you, Lord, for Your faithful care
And for letting me know that you were there
Taking care of my daughter so very small.
Lord, thanks for being LORD of all!

©Dede Toney

God's Mercy

*H*ave you ever been in a bad situation and you told the Lord if He got you out of this one, you would do better and be better next time? Well, that was my prayer. I now had three girls, and they were pretty close in age. My oldest daughter Melissa was now four, Michelle two, and Melinda seven months. I was three months pregnant, and you know what I wanted. Yes, a boy! I had not given up on that request. In fact, I questioned if I should ask for a boy, but I kept requesting one anyway. I went to the Doctor to have a sonogram. I really did not want to know what the baby was, but then again, it was going to help me plan better in terms of clothes. When we arrived at the office, the doctor and nurses all knew what we wanted; after all, we had been there three times before. They prepared me for the sonogram and as we all looked at the screen, the nurse had this funny look on her face. She did not really want to tell me anything. She kept saying that the baby was hiding and she could not get a true picture of what it was. Then minutes later, the baby moved, and she was able to see. "Congratulations, you are having another girl." My heart sank. I tried not to show my disappointment. I whispered, "Lord, did You forget me? What's wrong with me? Please, Lord I know you are able. Have I not been faithful enough. Is that it? If not, what then?" After leaving the doctor's office, I felt God had rejected me. I did not understand. Maybe God felt I did not need a boy, so I had my girls pray. I felt that God would hear their innocent prayers and answer them. As time was drawing near to my delivery, my desperation increased. I pleaded, "Lord, please give me a son. I will take this baby anyway You give it to me as long as it is a boy." So, do you know what the Lord did? For the next couple of months, it seemed every show that I saw on TV was about couples who had been trying to have a baby. When they finally had one, something went wrong. I saw one show where this lady wanted a little girl. She already had two boys, and she finally conceived. The doctors were worried about her pregnancy because she had problems with her boys so they monitored her very closely. To make a long story short, she had a girl and this little girl was their angel. But the baby had a rare disease and was not expected to live more than a few months. After about three months, the baby died. Let me tell you; that is not all. The stories during those two months grew worse and my heart grew heavy. I was too scared to pray because of how selfish I had been in my prayers. I realized that I did not mean what I prayed. I did not want a boy any kind of way. By this time, I had stopped praying for anything. I felt that God was disappointed in me; after all, He had just helped me with my daughter Melinda, and here I was asking selfishly again. It was now May, and I was ready to deliver. Even though we all knew it was a girl, I was still somewhat disappointed, but I had accepted the fact that a girl must be best. We knew her name was going to start with an M, but we had not picked it out yet. I went into labor, but it was false. A few days went by and on May 25th my water broke. We went to the hospital and I received my epidural. While I was sitting there relaxing with Rob, all the monitors connected to the baby started screeching. The nurses rushed in and told my husband he had to leave so they could prep me for an emergency C-section because the baby was in distress. I could not believe it. I thought I was having a nightmare. It was happening again. This time the baby's cord was too long and it was wrapped around the foot causing the heart rate to go down. I had no prayers to pray, and I did not know what to say. I was completely emotionless. I felt that it was my fault because of how I had prayed.

Have you ever been like that before, so numb you could not respond? All the verses I knew in the Bible came to my heart, but I was too emotionally weak to say them. They just flowed through my head. I could not even cry, but somehow tears streamed down my face. I was not crying. At least, I did not think I was. I believed the tears were words that I could not say like, "Lord I'm sorry. Here I am again in the same situation. I thought I learned last time. I didn't mean to repeat the same attitude. Help me in anyway You see fit." (Remember, these words were from my heart, not my on lips.) At that moment, I completely relaxed. Now, they had been monitoring the baby all the time so when we arrived at the labor room, the doctor approached my husband and me and told us that the baby's cord somehow loosened and I was going to be able to deliver normally. I just closed my eyes. God came through again and I whispered, "Thank You." As I began to push, the head of my baby emerged and the nurses and the doctor were encouraging me to give one more push. As the shoulders were released and they pulled the baby out, the doctor shouted, "IT'S A BOY!" A boy! No way! Could it be true? Was I dreaming? They had to show him to me for me to believe it was a boy. Remember that I told you I went into labor May 25th. Well, that was my birthday. God went beyond my request even in my selfishness and even when I was at my weakest. He gave me the desires of my heart. He wrapped my son with His love, and as the doctor placed him on my chest, I felt like it was God saying to me, "Happy Birthday, daughter. I love you."

After all that drama, I now know what the Initial M stood for when we were trying to pick a girl's name. It stood for "MERCY." You see, I deserved the treatment of someone who took God for granted. Instead, He showed me His unconditional love. I deserved the consequences of someone who was faithless, yet He remained faithful. He gave the opposite of what I really should have received. The gift of my son had nothing to do with me. It was all about the Lord and what He wanted for me. You may say, "Well, He did not give me the desires of my heart; in fact, He has not answered any of my prayers the way I want them to be answered." All of that may be true, but here is something to bank on and that is God's gifts and blessings are always perfect. They are just what we need. We may never understand why He chooses to act in the way He does, but it is always for a purpose. Nothing God gives us is a waste. It always serves a divine purpose EVERYTIME!

So what if this is your case? Keep seeking after His heart. Remember, you need to know what He likes so you will know what kinds of things to pray for because EVERYTHING was made for His KINGDOM AGENDA!

My friends, over 2000 years ago God gave us His only begotten Son. He was wrapped in swaddling clothes, and thirty-two years later He was forced to carry a cross on His shoulders. Men nailed Him to it. As He gave His very life, He was saying He loved us and forgave us. I enjoyed my son the moment he lay on my chest, and I have enjoyed him ever since, but his life will not give me or him eternal life. Only Christ, God's Son, can do that. Accept God's Son so you will enjoy a spiritual birthday, one that will last for eternity. Out of this experience I wrote a poem entitled, "God's Mercy." It was written as if God were talking to me about my special day.

Do not let your life be overpowered by selfish wants. Instead, let God's Son give you the power to want what He wants. No, you will not start off that way, asking for what He wants, but you want Him to help you get to that point. I made many mistakes in that area, and I am still making them, but inspite of myself, He came through every time. However, sin did, too. The good thing is that I knew where to go. I knew He was Almighty and that He knew what was best even though I did not act like it. "Me" got in the way.

Readers, it will be your own individual relationship with the Lord that will help you to want what He wants, and that kind of relationship comes from growing in the knowledge of who He is. **The more of Him you know, the less of you, you will need.** Let me say it again. **The more of Him you know, the less of you, you will need**. He wants to be your everything. Believe me, He is able to carry that load.

God's Mercy
Happy Birthday

My Dear Child...

Another year I give to you, to serve Me with your heart.

Another year to remind you that I will never part.

Another year to guide you, and show you that I care.

Another year to stretch you and to make you well aware

That I am God your Father who loves you very much.

And want you to get to know Me and experience My loving touch.

Yes, you will encounter trials, and struggles along life's way,

but just read and trust My word and remember the things I say.

For I am also mighty, willing and able too

to answer the prayers you have for Me and victoriously come through.

So as you celebrate this birthday, I hope you'll always know,

that I am your Heavenly Father, to whom you can always go.

Love Your Heavenly Father

© Dede Toney

Just Like You

Four children, a husband and I made up our family of six. It was scary. You see, having children was not the hard part. Raising them right was the challenge. I remember sitting at home one day overwhelmed at the thought. I called my mom because I needed to hear her voice. I needed the voice of an experienced woman who had done it well. She encouraged me, but her classic statement was, "Seek God's wisdom always!"

Here I was thinking I had to fill her shoes. Her shoes were not what she wanted me to fill. She wanted me to seek God's way even if it meant standing alone. Parents, when was the last time you gave your son or daughter that advice? Free yourself, take the pressure off of you, and direct them back to the Father. He is an awesome parent with first hand experience. That night I tucked my four children into bed, read them a bedtime story and prayed with them. When I left the room, I wrote a poem called, "Just like you."

Just Like You

As I raise my children everyday,
Remind me, Father, that I must pray.
That I would raise them all for Thee
Being a Godly model for them to see.
Help me teach them all Your ways
And encourage them to serve You all their days.
But most of all let them see You
In what I say and in what I do.

©Dede Toney

Thank You, Friends

*T*here is nothing one has accomplished or has been successful at without a friend or friends along the way. I have had many people who have crossed my path. Each of them has given me treasures in my life, but there are five friends who have been with me in the times of my life where what they had, God knew I needed THEN!

Have you ever had those friends that stuck by you through thick and thin, those you could share whatever was on your heart and know you would not be judged by it? Those who stayed up late nights listening to your worries and at times comforting you and wiping away the tears? Well, I would like to share those friends with you. I am convinced that God allows people to cross our paths to draw us closer to Him. Each of the people that I am going to share added much richness to my life in a time when I sought Him most. It has not all been a pleasant experience, but necessary, and for these friends, I am thankful.

This friend has been with me for twenty-two years. She knew me before I got married; in fact, she came to Alabama to see me get married. She was also there through the births of all my children. No matter the issue or concern of my life, she has been there for me. What I have gleaned from this friend is the **importance of building others up.** She was very encouraging and a supportive friend who mentored me as a new bride and mom. Her favorite words to me everyday were "I'm so proud of you." She does not know how much esteem that gave me over the years and even now. Thank you, MaryAnn Tennison, for your kindness and support that have encouraged me to walk like Christ in my marriage and as a mom.

My next friend taught me **how to balance my life**. She held me accountable for spending time with the Lord and balancing my time between church and home. She walked me through issues about Christ that I did not understand. For ten solid years, I met at her house and we wrote down our goals, and we held each other accountable. She taught me how to prostrate myself before the Lord and petition Him. She always said, "YOU have to want to live for the Lord. That has to be YOUR heartbeat." Her words of wisdom to me were, "YOU win or lose by the way YOU choose." I have found that statement to be true. Thank you, Elizabeth Cannings, for your patience with me as I grew and for always directing me towards Christ. You gave me fuel for the race.

The value of friendship is what I learned from my next friend. I have often had difficulty in this area. Either I spend too much time or not enough time being a friend; I do not seem to get it right. This friend has been there no matter what. I can honestly say she loves me unconditionally. She has been an ear for my children, a great listener and comforter, but most of all, she availed herself to me, always watching out for me in everything. She is like that battery; she keeps going and going and going. "She would say, "Life is too short to hold on to hurts and pains that others do against you. Love them and move on. Think about it. Christ could have held our sins against us but chose to forgive us and continue to love, support and care for us. I have found we need a friend most when we least deserve one. Debra Taylor, thank you, for trusting God to lead you in modeling friendship. You have been a valuable role model to me. Thanks for your constant forgiveness and your unfailing love for me. I have treasured them in my heart.

My next friend taught me the value of leadership. He showed me how to minister to people. "LOVE YOUR PEOPLE" was his motto. When you think about that word "Love," it goes back to the definition of God's love. It is patient, it is kind, and it does not hold grudges. It is wanting the best for the other person. It is walking with a person, helping to strengthen his weakness, and building up their strength. He understood that leadership meant spending time in the presence of God so we would know the needs of the people we are serving. He also encouraged me to dream big because I had a big

God! Gerard Davis, thanks for being a faithful friend who taught me how to dream in Christ. Your strong leadership and your unselfishness added richness to my life. I will never forget your kindness.

This next friend I am going to end with has taught me the value of **commitment**. She has five children, and we have gone through so many stages in our lives together. We had our children together and talked through mothering issues, marriage issues, and just life issues together. She has been a tower of strength for me. We have spent late nights, weekends, night drives, and many, many conversations on the phone about this life in Christ. Deborah McCampbell, I cannot begin to tell you how much I love you. Thank you for ALWAYS being there. Thanks for the laughter, the tears, and the pure shouts we have had over these past twenty-two years. Your commitment before the Lord has helped guide my steps as I continue to walk with Him.

The building up of others, a balanced life, friendship, leadership, and commitment are the critical building blocks that I needed in my life at the time I met these friends. These qualities were what I needed to continue my journey in Christ, and God graciously provided these role models for me.

Although these are five people I have shared, there have been many more who have blessed me. So to all of you, thank you. Thank you for your love, your advice, your prayers, your financial support, your friendships, and your patience. Thank you, even for those times when you lovingly had to confront me. Those acts of kindness kept my soles lubricated through the dry spell of walking with the Lord. I dedicate this next poem to all of you.

Thank You, Friends

Thank you, friends, for letting me see,
That there was potential inside of me.
Thank you, friends, for letting me know,
That no matter what, to you I could go.
Thank you, friends, for your listening ears
That helped to dry my many tears.
Thank you, friends, for your faithful ways,.
That got me through many difficult days.
Thank you, friends, for the friendship walks,
and the long, long hours of wisdom talks.
Thanks so much for making life grand,
And for being such caring and faithful
FRIENDS!
©Dede Toney

God's Grace

Snapshots A Plenty

Well readers, for many years God gave me snapshots a plenty. He took me from a teenager to accepting Him, to marrying, to having children, to acquiring friends, to now, growing deeper in the knowledge of Him.

I am learning though, that through the journey, there are many mountains and valleys. There are waiting rooms and drop-off points all intended to draw us closer to the Father. You have read God's Word that says, "His grace is sufficient." Grow to learn that. Nothing matters in this world but Him. As we walk the journey, He knows our fears, our weakness, and what we need to make us stronger. You see, we think no trials and no trouble make us stronger, but honestly, strength comes through weakness. You and I will never know how strong we are if we have never experienced a hard time. Anyone can be strong when the going is good, but can we still be strong when everything is falling apart? I remember hearing a song that said, "When you see me on my knees it's not because I'm weak, but I'm getting stronger." Believe me, you will have snapshots a plenty in the area of weakness, but do not lose heart. Just remember, trials are to remind you and me that no matter how successful or well known we are, we are NOTHING without HIM! He is enough. So, the next time life finds you on your knees, be thankful because that is your chance to **get stronger.**

God's Grace

Lord, looking out my window it's evident to see
that when I'm not thinking of You, You are thinking of me.
From the top of my head to the tip of my toes
You know all about the fears I hold.
But thank God it's you who knows all my fears
and who understands words when there's only tears.
You come to my aid when I'm feeling blue.
You continually show me that I'm valuable, too.
So when life finds me weak and burdens hard to bear,
I'm glad to know that You're always there!

©Dede Toney

"I Do"

I remember when Rob and I said "I do" on our wedding day. We gazed into each other's eyes, and we knew there was nothing in life we could not conquer together. For the next several years we tried to do just that. However, years passed and children came into the picture, and Rob and I found ourselves not doing too many things together. Finances started skyrocketing. Rob started experiencing pressures on the job and I was a homemaker and I felt pressures as well. Our only conversations were about bills and the kids. All the little things that we once did so well for each other to show our appreciation began to dwindle. Sound familiar? Believe me, we will all experience days like this in a marriage. I know as a couple we do not set out to drift apart, but when we find ourselves not praying, spending time or talking to each other about each other, that will happen.

I think marriage is wonderful, but it is no easy thing, yet I do know that two people with two opinions in the same house can have disagreements, but only God can make them one, and only love for Him and each other will keep them that way. There will be problems in marriage. Some small, some large, but believe me, there will be some. The greatest gift that a husband can give his wife is to seek the Lord daily on how to love her and then show her. The best gift that a wife can give her husband is to seek the Lord daily on how to encourage and respect him and then encourage and respect him. Yet the proof of their love is their service to each other, not just when things are going well, but when things are at their worst and falling apart. Everyday should be a day that we set out to serve each other, with the right motives and attitude. How will you know what your spouse wants or likes? ASK. Make it a point to be interested in what your spouse does each day. Make encouragement your mouth-piece and dedicate yourself to building up each other even in dispute. You see, the best gift we can give our children is a HOME not a building, but people who are Christ-centered. He did not say marriage would be easy. That is why He wants us to depend on Him. Remember, He is the perfect parent and marriage counselor. His ways are always right, and the results are quite victorious.

You may be having problems right now in your marriage. God knows, and He is not absent. I know at times it seems that He does not hear, but He does. Keep seeking Him. Keep trusting Him. His ways of doing things are never like we think, but the outcome is always just what we need.

This next poem was written while I was going through a trial in my own marriage. I wanted to change Robert to fit me instead of his being changed to fit God's agenda. So I asked God for a marriage that was pleasing to Him. Now that was not easy because that meant I had to die to self. Christ died to self did He not? When He was in the Garden of Gethsemane, He told God what He wanted, but He said, "Not my will but Your will be done." He wanted more of what the Father wanted than what He Himself wanted, and if our marriages are going to be successful, we must give Him permission to have His way!

"I DO"

Lord, we give you our marriage so that we could be,
all that we need in this marriage of three.
Help us to learn to serve and care
even when the feelings sometimes aren't there.
Assist us to see each other through you
especially when we're selfish and stubborn too.
May encouragement be our rap and integrity our race
As we love each other and seek Your face.
Lord be our center and our focus too
Because this marriage became three when we said "I do"

©Dede Toney

The Waiting Room

*B*een in a waiting room lately? They are all the same. Sometimes in the waiting room we may get there first and they call our name right away. Then there are times when we get in first and watch others who come later get called first. Or better yet, be on time waiting and someone with a bigger emergency gets bumped up before us. How about if we are there, and it is almost our time to be called and the doctor receives an emergency call from the hospital. Whatever the case, waiting is not an easy thing to do.

Many of us are waiting for the Lord to do things in our lives whether with our health, our families, relationships, careers, or spiritual life. Whatever the situation, we all must enter the waiting room. We will be called, in God's time. As we wait, we will see people come after us and get blessed while we still wait. We might even experience tragedy in the waiting room as we watch others triumph. We may find ourselves questioning if God even notices that we are waiting or if He has forgotten about us.

As I have encountered the waiting room, I've noticed two things will happen. We will either grow or we will wither there. It sounds funny, but it is true. It will all depend on our focus. Now, Satan's job is to keep our eyes on the wait and not on THE WAY. He wants us to feel hopeless, not hopeful. Satan has a way of getting us to feel like a victim, but God wants us to realize we are victors in Him. How we focus, my friends, will help our time in the waiting room be endurable. Have you noticed that doctors' have soft music and books to keep us occupied while we wait. It is designed to keep our mind off the wait. Knowing what God is like and what His Word says about Him helps to keep us while we wait. We should fill our mind with His Word. He is faithful, He is all-powerful, He never tires, His grace is sufficient, and He is able. Let these thoughts lubricate your mind while you wait. Oh yes, we will get distracted, we will grumble, we will complain, we will question what God is doing, and we may even lose heart and fall away because the wait is too long. If this occurs, come back, because when our name is called, and our name will be called, He will give us personal service and the solution will be tailor made. Hide the Word in your heart, and fellowship with other believers while you wait. Seek out testimonies because that is what boosts you and gives you energy to stay. Now, while you wait, do not go comparing your situation to those in the waiting room or your blessings to others. Trust the Lord and remember that His ways are not your ways nor His thoughts your thoughts. He will do the absolute best for you and for me, even though we may not feel His loves while He does it.

So what do we do while we wait? Keep praying and trusting. Do not stop fellowshipping with other believers because what you will find in the waiting room is people worse off than you. Have you ever thought that maybe you are there to be a blessing for someone else's life? Your mission in the waiting room just might be to save a life, encourage a life or be a light while you wait. Now do not get me wrong. It is tough in the waiting room, and many times we are angry while we are there, but as I said before, you will do one of two things, grow or wither. He has not left you. Remember, He knows everything. Nothing, I mean nothing, catches Him off guard. You are not operating with an inexperienced physician or counselor. You are seen by the ALMIGHTY! The next several pages contain poems about the waiting room.

Are you weary? Have you been waiting a long time? Don't lose heart. Be encouraged because His answer will be on time.

Life's Waiting Room

Lord, I'm in life's waiting room, waiting for Your care.
Did you know I've been waiting?
Do You know how long I've been there?
Have You heard me crying? Have You seen my tears?
After talking He assured me He'd been there for years.
"I love you, my child, and I have heard your prayer
and I'd never give you more than you could bear.
Each time that you enter is to make you strong.
It's to build your character so you can go on.
For My yoke is easy and My ways are kind.
And whatever you need, it will be on time.
So each time that you enter, waiting for My care
Don't look around to see, who else is waiting there.
Don't judge or draw conclusions about their reason's why
because everyone must enter and must wait for Me to supply!

©Dede Toney

ARE YOU WRESTLING WITH BEING SINGLE?
DON'T WORRY, THE LORD UNDERSTANDS.
TRY ASKING HIM TO RE-FOCUS YOUR THOUGHTS
TO HIM AND HIS WILL FOR YOU WHILE YOU WAIT
THIS POEM IS DEDICATED TO YOU.

Prayer For Single Christians

Lord, thank you for choosing someone like me.
To be a living vessel to glorify Thee.
In my single life, create in me
A hunger to know You more intimately.
Teach me, Father, to be content.
Don't let me fall for someone not sent
But let me trust Your ultimate will
And rest in Your love and learn to be still.
For I know that You haven't forgotten about me
And I know that You hear and I know that You see
The times that I'm lonely, sadden or down
Because there's so many married people around.
I also know that You've heard me sigh
Because at times I've felt You've passed me by.
But with all that I know and all that I've heard,
Help me trust Your promises I've read in Your word
Lord, To live this single life I'm gonna need Your help
I will need Your wisdom to guide my every step
So that I would not dwell on a husband or wife
But thirst to serve You only in my single Christian life.

Are you experiencing brokenness? Are your families falling apart? If so, do not give up or lose heart but enter into the presence of God and let Him be your Lord.

In His Presence

Lord, as I enter into Your presence, I humbly bow down to You.
Take me, break me, mold and show me, what it is I am to do.
I'm tired of pretending that I'm walking in Your way.
I need to hear from You, oh Lord, and I need to hear today.

I come into Your presence with families broken apart. Lord please,
let there be true repentance, so unity would be in our hearts.
Take each member of my family and even outsiders, too,
and cause our lives to be pure and Holy, always attractive to You.
Take all of our families and revive them through and through so that
We would be true testimonies of what You're able to do.

©Dede Dorsey

Dare To Be Yourself

*M*y children love to go places with their friends and sometimes they have friends over to visit. As my husband and I observed them with their friends in our home on several occasions, we noticed they were not consistent in enforcing our rules. We would ground them and punish them, but still no change. It seemed that they were willing to take the punishment rather than reveal to their friends that there were rules in our home. We confronted them and learned they were trying to fit in. They were trying to impress their friends so they would think my children had freedom to do as they pleased- basically NO RULES. We asked them if the world had no rules, would we be safe to function? Rules keep us safe. Having a standard about something gives us respect. We shared with them that friends do not respect us less because we have rules and standards; they respect us more. Now of course, they will never admit that openly, but we will see a difference in the way they treat us and value us. Sometimes we will be made fun of or be teased. I know it is difficult because everyone wants friends, but do not let that discourage you, and do not compromise YOURSELF to get them. This not only applies to children but to adults as well. This being yourself thing is not easy. So, how does one get through it? First, we must adopt God's opinion of ourselves. He says that "we are wonderfully and fearfully made." That means He took time with us. We were not just thrown together. Just think, He uniquely created us with gifts, talents and abilities to use for Him.

If you are a parent of a child who is having difficulty with self-esteem or is rebelling against your rules at home, keep praying for him. That is extremely important. Many times, no matter what we say, our children appear not be listening; they want to give us their opinion and no matter what we say, they tend to do the opposite. Keep standing for righteousness, and bringing them before the Lord. Keep bringing out the best in them even though you see their worst. Compliment them often and thank them when they have done what you have asked. You will find them trying to do right more often. It may not come for a while, but slowly you will see them trying to please you. Communicate with your children, and try not to communicate only when a punishment is in order. Compliment and encourage often. Is it difficult to do? You bet it is, especially when they show us so much of the behavior opposite to what we are expecting. Try not to get caught up in the BEHAVIOR. Instead, focus on the SAVIOR who is able to shape them and mold them. Remember, children will always try to impress, but if we give them roots and nourish their character with prayer and praise along with love and **discipline,** we will begin to see them grow. Now remember, growing is a process. That is what I have to keep telling myself. Each stage is different, but what will give them stability is that we stand as their parents. We owe them that. I promise you they will appreciate you so much more for it. We should not shortchange our children but help them become what is pleasing to God, not just what is pleasing to us. God took pride in making us. We need to help them value pride in themselves by encouraging them to stand up for what they know is right. How do we do it? Staying on our KNEES and BEING THERE FOR THEM!

Dare To Be Yourself

Have you ever wanted to disappear or just be someone else?
If so, this poem is to encourage you to try and be yourself.
You may have had words hurt you or you may feel you don't fit in,
But you and yourself are great, believe me,
you are your best friend.
you know your every feelings, you know the things you want,
Don't let others try to change you, just be bold and say "I won't."
I won't be disrespectful; I won't cheat to win.
I won't compromise myself in order to fit in.
I won't continue to waste my life as I watch time slowly go by.
I want to make a difference; I want the chance to try.
I do have ideas to offer and I'm really an ok friend.
I do have people who love me and are cheering for me to win.
So I'll take this challenging dare, and prove to everyone else
That the greatest gift I can give anyone, is the joy of being myself!

© Dede Toney

Time With My Father

Can you remember the fondest moment(s) you have shared with your father, grandfather, uncle or male guardian? I do. My fondest memory occurred when I was in the 5th grade. My mom had just had twin girls, which made it nine children. One day my dad was going on a short business trip. I saw him packing a few clothes and I asked him where he was going. He said he was going to Atlanta on business, but he was going to stop over and see his parents for the weekend. I wanted to go so badly, but I knew mom needed me there. After all, it had not been long since the twins were born; therefore, I did not ask. Well, my dad came to me that night and asked me if I wanted to go with him to visit Grandma and Grandpa. I was speechless. I could not say "yes" fast enough. I did not tell my sister, Freda, because I did not want to run the risk of her asking Dad if she could go, too.

I packed my clothes and was so excited that I could not sleep that night. The next day Dad and I set out for Atlanta, Georgia. I was ecstatic. I was finally alone with my father, just he and I in the car. I sat back and watched the mountains and the sunrise. After being on the road awhile, we began to talk. I did not know that he knew so much about me and what I had been going through. I was shocked. I thought he never noticed my fears, knew my dreams or knew when I was sad. Our relationship was not very close because he was so strict and I felt that he was so into my following his daily rules that he did not have a clue about how I felt each day. For the first time, I saw him in a different light. He actually was tuned in to my feelings, not all of them, but at least it was a start. We talked and cleared up misunderstandings and really had a wonderful time.

That time with my father was priceless, and it was not until I was alone with him that I could hear him and better understand his role as my father. That is the way it is with our Heavenly Father. Our best understanding of who He is comes when we spend quality time with Him alone. He wants a relationship with us that will draw us into obedience to Him. He is not trying to force us to love Him or serve Him. He wants us to have a desire to get to know Him better. He wants us to understand His role as our father and faithful friend.

Fathers, you are so important in the lives of your children. They may never say anything to you. Things may even seem ok, but believe me, your presence and responses are critical. You help shape an image of a God we cannot see. If you never tell your children you love them or appreciate them, it is hard to convince them that God loves them and values them. If you never have time for your children or if you never talk to them, it becomes difficult for a child to trust that God wants to spend time with them or enjoys talking to them. Your relationship with your children sets the tone for any relationship they will encounter in their lives. My father was a man of his word. That has helped me so much in my life because it has helped me to trust a God that I could not see.

So you say you have blown it with your children. Maybe that is your case, but as long as you have life, there is always time to get it right. Instead of letting PRIDE be your garment, try PRAYING. Instead of GIVING up because you have not been there, try trusting God's GRACE to carry you back. Instead of forgetting because you have messed up, try forgiving yourself and allowing God to restore you. Remember, that is why He died. He knew we had these selfish ways, and His plan was to give us victory over them through His death and resurrection instead of their having victory over us!

Listen, do not be overwhelmed if your family does not want you back or your children resent you and do not ever want to see you again. CONSISTENCY in your walk with the Lord and your relationship with Him will be your testimony of change, not your words. Once you have been faithful in that, let God be God!! Just keep seeking Him, and in His time and in His way, you will be comforted. In the meantime, ask Him to help you become more like Him and accept the molding process. I promise He will do it. TRUST HIM!

Guess what? If you do not have a personal relationship with Christ as Lord and Savior, you are too weak to get it right. You do not even have God's perspective on Fatherhood, so you have lost already, but if you give your life to the Lord, He will restore you and give you back those years that you have lost. He is there waiting for you. He wants to show you how to be a Father. He is the MASTER and the best FATHER to seek!

Time With My Father

I never knew I could feel so safe until I spent time with You.

I never knew inspite of my heart You wanted to grow closer, too.

So many times I didn't know how great Your love could be

Until I spent time alone with You and

realized You've always loved me.

You loved me when I didn't listen and no matter the things I'd done.

You loved me and You proved it when you gave up your only Son.

You loved me enough to give your Spirit to help me everyday.

You loved me no matter what, and You never turned me away!

Father, thank you for spending time with me.

Thank you for your care.

Thank you for daily showing me that You'll never stop being there!

©Dede Toney

Good-bye

*I*t was a Saturday morning in July of 2002 and I had just hosted a retreat at my house. After the retreat, the boys went to Six Flags, and the rest of my children dispersed in different directions. I decided to go walking after a long peroid of typing on my book, and I left our dog Oreo and my husband sleeping on the couch. Now, let me tell you about Oreo. She was a cocker spaniel that my daughter Melissa brought home from college. I was always afraid of dogs so I knew this dog thing was not going to work. I ran from the dog everyday for a month. Then one day I stopped running because I realized she was not worried about me at all. She ran the house. She had everyone else at her beck and call, especially my husband. They grew very close and inseparable. Whenever my husband went out of town, Oreo slept on his pajamas. She would not eat, and she moped all the time. And when he went to work, she slept with her head buried in his tennis shoes. She loved the kids, and they grew to love her more everyday. Well, on this particular day, Oreo was into everything. She grabbed at our shoes, licked our feet, barked at the vacuum cleaner or ran and jumped on the couch just for attention. But after all these activities, she decided to go to sleep on the couch with Rob. I went to the park and after about an hour had passed, I checked my phone to see if I had any calls and sure enough my husband had called. He told me that a friend came to visit and he went out to greet him. Oreo ran out of the house behind him, and at the same time she ran out the house, a truck was coming down the street. Oreo always barked at the trucks, but this time she darted out into the street and the truck ran over her. My husband, in disbelief, swept her up and rushed her to the animal hospital where they took X-rays. The doctor told him that she had multiple internal injuries and that her condition was poor. How could things happen so fast? I had just left her and she was running and playing and getting into everything. My baby daughter was with my husband and had talked to my second daughter Michelle. Michelle was visiting a friend and called me from there crying uncontrollably. I went and picked her up, as well as my son who had returned home from Six Flags. He did not know about Oreo, but when he saw Michelle in the car crying he asked what had happened. When I told him, he became very quiet while we made our way to the animal hospital. When we entered the room where Oreo was, she cried. She was so happy to see us. She laid her head on our arms, licking us and loving on us. Let me tell you, there was not a dry eye in the room. The vet told us what it would take to save her. They shared the procedures with us as well as the charges. It was more than we had. I knew right then we could not afford to save her. We had two teenagers getting ready to go to college as well as a junior and sophomore in high school who were very active in sports. But that moment was excruciating. My heart was so heavy. Here I had finally adjusted to the dog and loved her very much, and now we were faced with the decision of saving her or putting her to sleep. After discussing it together, we knew we had to put her to sleep. "How can things change so quickly," my middle daughter Michelle asked as she cried? Oreo was still so happy as she rubbed her. "Mom, please save her," my son cried out. "Please don't put her to sleep. We love her, we love her. Look at her, Dad. She is so happy. She doesn't know what's getting ready to happen to her. Please, Mom and Dad. Please don't let her die." The reality was, we could not afford to save her. We finally gave permission for them to put her to sleep. We all said our last good-byes and left her there.

When we arrived home and walked in our door, we were so accustomed to Oreo jumping on us and crying because she was so happy that we all began to cry all over again. We cried all night. Rob and I missed her sleeping beside our bed at night and waking us up every morning at 5:00 to go outside. The toys that she chewed were so clearly visible. The memories of her were everywhere.

My friends, this day was a teachable moment. You see, my children had never experienced death that closely. They loved Oreo, and as far as they were concerned, she was ok. In reality, she was messed up internally.

Do you know that without Christ, we are internally messed up and no one has the means to fix us? We had to put Oreo to death in order to free her from the pain she was experiencing from the injuries, and the reality is, we will NEVER see her again. She will become only a memory in our hearts forever. We have an internal injury called SIN. When we do not have Christ in our lives, we are powerless and unable to be victorious. You see, we could not tell from the outside that Oreo was hurt when we first walked in because she was full of excitement and happiness to see us, but internally she was messed up. And unless she had an operation, she would die. The injuries would not just disappear. For us, God saw the internal injury, SIN, and came up with a plan in Jesus. He was the only one who said, "I will pay the cost to fix them." I wanted so much for someone to say that to us the day Oreo was injured. We wanted someone to say, "We will pay the bill in full and you can keep your dog." But no one did.

No one stood before God and said, "I will pay the cost" except Jesus. We had to say goodbye to our dog. Please do not let someone have to say goodbye to you forever. They will, if you die without Christ. He is the only physician who can forever free you from your internal injury. You will have to die to self, but you will be made alive through Christ. The choice is yours. The good news is that it is FREE! He loves you, my friend, and His utmost desire is for you to live with Him forever.

If you know the Lord, our number one job is to make sure others come to know Him, too. We must all be about sharing the gospel. Do not settle for "goodbye." Let the words be, "See you later." Jesus is more than wonderful. He is the lifesaver, the internal physician. Please, share this lifesaving news TODAY because that friend, co-worker or loved one just might not see tomorrow.

Goodbye

Take a little time to tell someone that Jesus died for them.
Take a little time to give someone hope when life is dim.
Take the life God's given you as a result of Jesus His son
And spread the gospel in everyplace and share it with everyone.
Don't let your days get busy, with empty kinds of stuff.
A life is depending on the gospel to share His news is a must.
So what if they call you religious, so what if they laugh at you too.
Jesus went all the way to Calvary because He was in love with you.
He didn't say it would be easy He just wants us to try
Because if we get too busy the word we'll hear is "goodbye."

©Dede Toney

Life's Focus

*E*ver felt like giving up and throwing in life's towel? I have been there so many times, and what bothers me is that I find myself there more often than I would like. Pressures from finances, raising children, job and marital strains have kept me paralyzed and not moving in my walk with the Lord. Thank God for mercy, which is fresh and new everyday. Sometimes when we fall on our knees, saying the same things and asking forgiveness for the same sins, I wonder if God gets tired of our redundancy. I wonder if He shakes His head in disappointment of our behavior everytime we approach His throne. I wonder if He feels like giving up on us. Well, my friends, those are the exact questions Satan wants us to ponder so that he can paint God to be a conditional loving Father. He wants us to dwell on our weakness and stay there, never accepting God's forgiveness and love which moves us back into obedience and fellowship. What I am learning to do is to focus on what really matters to God. It is not DUTY that He wants to draw us to repentance and righteousness, it is a DESIRE. He does not want us to LABOR in our quest to please Him; He wants it to be our LOVE. So, do not get caught dutifully and laboriously serving God. Let DESIRE and LOVE turn you around.

Life's Focus

Whenever life seems to get you down,
Don't despair just turn around.
'Cause when you turn your focus to
The Lord and King who created you,
You'll find more strength than ever before
And He'll help you walk through any door.
So trust Him for what you want to do
'Cause when He works, it's victory for you.

©Dede Toney

Slow Me Down, Lord

When I went into leadership at my church, Oak Cliff Bible Fellowship, I was eager and ready. I had asked the Lord to give me a vision for children's worship, and He did. In the early stages, I was talking to God every day. I was seriously making Him the center of the ministry. I prayed for the right people and He sent me three people-William Pearson, Gloria Delaney and my husband Robert. The four of us were excited to share the gospel with the children. We thought of so many creative ideas and visual things to help kids understand the gospel and have fun while learning. We four had a wonderful three years. Then I found myself consulting God less. Everything began to fall apart. I stopped doing what made us strong- praying. I stopped doing what made us unified, and that was practicing before the service. I did not continue to give the ministry to the Lord, and it fell apart and became a program. I realized God's word when He said, "Apart from Him we can do nothing." I allowed it to become a program of people instead of a ministry for God. Does this sound familiar? If so, do not be ashamed, change. Refocus. Place the Operator back in the front, and you follow His orders. Remember, it is His ministry and He knows what it needs to make it go and keep it running. DO NOT try to do it without HIM; it WILL NOT work. Ask the Lord to lead and guide you. That is what I did as I wrote this next poem.

Is your ministry falling apart? Are your people drained because you care more about the program than them? If so, ask the Lord what He wants you to do. Tell Him you cannot do this without Him and confess for trying to do it on your own. My prayer was:

"SLOW ME DOWN." Do not let me dash ahead of You. Direct my thoughts and give me wisdom as I lead. Help me to be sensitive to the needs of the people in my care and help me never to become too big to serve them." Oh, believe me, I failed many times even though I prayed, but God did not give up on me. He kept blessing and blessing inspite of me. He will do that for you, too. You see, when I saw that I had Him as a PASSENGER, not MY PILOT, I realized why everything was so hard. If you are a pastor or leader, give your ministry to the Lord. Give your flock to the Lord and remember, without the Master's leading, it will just be a program or a building.

Slow Me Down Lord

Being in the ministry, Lord, so many times I'm racing
To conquer all its problems that I am daily facing.
But slow me down, Lord, so I can plainly see
That these are Your people and this is Your ministry.
For You will give wisdom if only I would ask
And You will give me endurance to successfully complete the task.
So go before me, Father, and show me what to do
Because I want to be ministering in a way
that ultimately pleases You.

© Dede Toney

God's Church

When I think of all that is going on in the world, prayer is all we have that will help. We should pray that more people come to know the Lord and then pray for those who know the Lord, to remain faithful as His light in the world. **Everyone needs prayer**.

Sometimes I think we forget that pastors need prayer. They hurt just like we do. They have family issues like we do and need support as well. Sometimes we need to just say "thank you" to our pastors and let them know we appreciate their commitment to the Lord and their service to us. As the flock, we should continue to pray that the Lord will protect our pastors and guard them from evil people.

This chapter is dedicated to my pastor, Dr. Anthony T. Evans, and all pastors who preach the Word and bear the burden of the flock daily. Dr. Evans, thank you for making the lives of people important to you. Over and over, you share the seriousness of salvation in that it is a matter of spiritual life or death. I have grown for twenty-two years under your leadership, and I appreciate not only your presentation of the gospel, but I value the fact that you want the gospel to become a lifestyle. You are not interested in just the mere words of God, but in the spirit of God working in our lives. You challenged me as a member to do two things: **grow fat** in studying the Word and **grow up** by applying it daily. I accepted the challenge and I realized that growing fat and growing up are what impact people and change lives.

I have grown and learned so much under your leadership, and I would like to thank you for being a powerful man of the Lord whose life and commitment are steadfast. Thank you for being an authentic testimony and an exceptional role model to me in my Christian life.

The greatest gift a congregation can give to a pastor is to grow deep in its relationship with the Lord, to have a willing heart to serve others and to model the gospel with its lives. If a pastor can lead his flock in that direction, it will definitely impact the world.

Prayer For The Flock

Lord, help our church be a church that's real,
not a building that houses people.
Help our church be a light on a hill, not a building with a steeple.
Don't let us be filled with only knowledge,
but a daily devotion to You
Knowing no matter our trials, You'll always see us through.
Give us Your kind of wisdom, and let us not compromise with sin,
but keep us pure and holy, so our lifestyles can draw people in.
Help us not to sit down, and get too comfortable to be,
faithful servants all around, moving to be used by Thee.
Father, help us to be kingdom-minded as we live this Christian life
Knowing there's nothing that You can't do cause
Your Son paid the ultimate price.
And if we're to be Your church and have Your light abound,
Please help us not to embarrass You, but impact the world around.

©Dede Toney

Leaving For College

I will never forget the first time we took our oldest daughter Melissa to college. We all were so proud of her and excited about her new adventure of independence, yet as parents, we questioned if we had properly prepared her, not for college, but for life. Had we instilled God's Word in her? Had we equipped her enough so that she could properly take care of herself? Were we there to answer questions about boys, relationships and other issues that she had? I think our most frightening concern involved her going to college and possibly doing the opposite of how her dad and I had taught her or getting in with the wrong group of people. If you have children in college, I know you understand my concern. My parents shared with me they had some of the same concerns, but they had to rest in the fact that they had done all that they could do. They had to place us in God's protective care and allow Him to direct us. They had already taught us how to pray and go before the Lord, just as we had done with our daughter. My parents had to trust that we would model it, and they were so right. We had to give our daughter to the Lord and trust that she would take what had been taught her and live it. So if you are asking yourself those same questions, remember that God is bigger and able to handle the job. So give your college student to HIM.

A College Prayer

As you prepare to go to college to be on your own,
We pray that you'd use the seeds that we've sown.
We've given you God's Word and we've modeled it to you
The things you should know and the things you should do
So that when you face trials or can't find your way
Just know Christ is able to keep you each day.

©Dede Toney

Finish It!

I am a part of a women's soccer team called the Lion Spurs, and we play soccer in the fall and the spring. We practice every week on the plays the coach has designed for us. Before the game, our coach huddles us up and gives us his expectation of the game. Even though we try to play as he instructs us, we do not always do what he asks, but that never keeps him from repeating it to us. When the game is in progress and one of the forwards or halfbacks is in position to shoot, we can hear him from the sidelines yelling, "Finish It." What he is saying is? Shoot with confidence. Strike the ball with power so it will be difficult for the opponent to intercept it.

You and I are in the game of life. Jesus is our coach, and He huddles us and He calls the plays. He gives us His expectations, and if we forget, we have His Word to remind us. He gives us our personal assignments, and He never gives us an assignment without equipping us. He is in the winning business. Even though we do not do as He asks, He does not stop asking. His desire is that we read the Word, His play book for daily living, practice it in our daily situations, and continue our fellowship with Him. He already knows all the plays. He has studied our opponent, Satan, and has put out all his fiery darts. The only way Satan can be victorious is if we believe him over Jesus. What is important in this game of life is that we recognize the voice of our coach, Jesus Christ. That comes from talking to Him everyday and being still long enough for Him to talk to us. He calls this "fellowship." Remember, Satan coaches, too, and his ways seem great, but the end result is destruction. Jesus coaches, but we can always recognize Him because everything He says is righteous, and the end result is victorious. What I like about Jesus the coach is that He does not just coach; He cheers as well. He is there when we are down and He is there when we are on top. When we get hurt in life's game, He treats the wounds and places us back in the game. When we cannot go anymore, He surrounds us with other believers to give us strength. He never leaves us alone. He will always be there cheering on the side lines. For Him, every-one plays. His goal is that everyone faithfully finishes.

Finish It!

No matter your call in life or what life takes you through,
You'll always have Satan who wants the worse for you.
He knows where you are weakest and he lures you gently
All in the name of pleasures, and when you fail, he quickly flees.
But he knows your Lord and Savior and He knows what Jesus can do
So he gets us all distracted by complaining and not trusting too.
He gets you and me so busy and centered on ourself
That we don't pray to God or try to help anyone else.
He tells us we are hopeless, we are losers and that we can't win.
He gets us totally focused on our terrible and horrible sin.
But I am here to tell you Jesus came and paid it all.
The big, the bad, and ugly, no matter how it's called.
God knew we all had sin and fallen short of Him.
He knew without His grace our lives would all be grim.
So He promised us a savior who would wash our sins away.
And wouldn't hold them against us He'd forgive us everyday.
But If you have not accepted what Christ did for you
You're powerless to say no, to the things Satan wants you to do.
But if Him, you have accepted, and His payment for your sin,
"Finish it!" Would be His words to you, cause with Him you'll
always win. Now, sometimes you'll get weary,
frustrated and want no more,
But what we must remember, is with Christ we'll always score.

©Dede Toney

The Course

*A*fter our soccer season is over in the spring, we usually take some time off in the summer to work out and keep in shape for the fall season. This past summer, we did not really plan a work-out session; everyone pretty much did her own thing. Some did water aerobatics while others of us met at the park and walked. One day while at the park, I saw my coach. He was on the track, walking the course. The course consists of workstations, slopes, curves, hills and straight-aways. He is familiar with the course because he brisk walks and runs four miles every day. He was really into it that day, and it showed by his drenched shirt and the sweat that dropped from his head and arms. I thought to myself, "I hope he doesn't expect me to walk the course like he does." I hated to walk and I was not interested in speed walking or working the different stations. All I wanted to do was be able to tell my soccer team that I worked out this summer by walking the track.

One day I had just gotten to the park, trying to walk early, and who pulled up to the park seconds later? You guessed it, my coach. He asked me if I wanted to walk the course with him. I hesitatingly said I would, but he also told me not to feel badly if he went off and left me behind. He was not joking either. He actually went off and left me. I could not keep up. But every now and then, I heard him yelling in the distance, "Keep going." Well, after watching him run the course for a while, I started the next day, walking without him. I wanted to build up my endurance so that when he asked me to walk with him again, I could keep up. It was awhile before I saw him again at the park, but when I did get a chance to run the course with him, I kept up. Weeks passed and I did not see him, but I kept running and when I did see him in passing, I told him I was still running the course and doing it under an hour. A month passed, and I was still running; sometimes my friends would come and run with me. The first thing I told them was not to feel badly if I left them. I was on a mission to finish under an hour. The next time I saw my coach, he was doing sit-ups in the sit-up station. I did not even ask any questions but just kept running. Later when I encountered him at the park, he and some other players were starting their run so I ran the course with them. "Now that you have the course down, you need to challenge yourself and do the stations. Pick one or two and work on them through the course" were his words. I started complaining and giving him all kinds of excuses, but he never skipped a beat. He just kept to the course and did his stations. I was a little offended because he showed no compassion or sympathy. He went off and left us, but I could hear him in the distance yelling, "work the course."

Our spiritual life is like a course. Sometimes we walk it and other times we run, but whether we walk or run, we must all stick to it. In the beginning we will not move fast. In fact, at first we may drag along, moaning and groaning and giving the Lord every excuse why we cannot make it. My friend, time does not wait until we start the course. It just ticks away. The longer we delay walking with the Lord, the harder life's struggles become. So how will we know our spiritual course? By practicing first with the Master and letting Him reveal it to us. Once we know His course for our lives, we must practice. If you don't know, keep seeking Him for it. When He feels we are progressing, He will add to the course. When he sees we are growing weary, He will give us His strength to finish it. Remember, the course is to be followed until He calls us home. There will be slopes, curves, hills, straight-aways, and, yes, work stations all along the way. God's journey for us is designed to make us spiritually strong. God's will for us is important, and we cannot allow our friends who do not want to know Him draw us away from the course. If we find ourselves off the course, just come back quickly because time is ticking. One day He will call us home. Will we be ready? Will we finish the course? Will He be pleased?

The Course

This course, oh Lord, is long and hard.
Help me to put on my spiritual guard.
Each piece You've given will help me to be

Courageous and ready to be used by Thee
Oh Lord, you are all I'll ever need.
U-are my strength, my reason for being
Rid my thoughts of doubt each day
So I will walk the course Your way
Every step I take or mile I run
LET IT BE PLEASING TO THEE,
TILL MY WORK IS DONE!
©Dede Toney

"I Will Never Leave You"

We have come to the end of *Glimpses of God's Faithfulness*, but we have not come to the end of His love. There is so much more I want to share about my Lord.

When I sit back and think about His love, I am drawn to tears wondering why would a Holy God want to be bothered with a sinner like me? What makes Him want to talk to me, spend time with me, bless me, care for me secure me, hold me, provide for me? What would cause Him to want me? I keep coming back to the words He used in John 3:16 -"For God so LOVED the world." It is His LOVE that wants us. It is His LOVE that keeps loving and forgiving us. It is His LOVE that sustains us from day to day. He promises never to leave us or forsake us. His light will never grow weary nor will it ever lose its power.

So whatever your situation, your finances, your marriage problems, your career, that terminal illness, that wayward child, that relationship, He WILL NEVER LEAVE YOU.

I want to end my book the way I started it, with "The Son." I have been with Him now for twenty-two years and through the journey, He has never let me down. Oh, He has done many things that were opposite of what I thought I needed, but His ways have always proven best. His ways have not always been easy, but He has always provided the means, the source, and the power to do the task. He does not promise to reveal His will to us all at once. That is where faith becomes important. We must trust Him with ALL our heart. THAT IS NOT EASY, BUT IT IS NECESSARY. That is why our fellowship with Him must be a priority. His ways and His character

MUST become important to us. I know this is not easy in a world that so often leaves Him out, but He is OUR ONLY HOPE! In my life He has been all-powerful; He has been everything that I have needed. I do not know what your life holds, but I do know He holds your life. He will not let you down and He will always come through. This last poem I wrote has given me fuel for the race and has brought comfort to my heart. I entitled it, "I Will Never Leave You," which is His promise to us. Rest on these words; they can save many years of worry and heartaches. It will not be easy, but when the race is over and you stand before the king and He says, "Well done," all the suffering will be worth it. For the race is not given to the swift but to them that endure until the end. My prayer is that this book has been an encouragement to you, to continue your journey with the LORD!

I Will Never Leave You

I love you My child,

With all of My heart.
I will take care of you.
Lo I'll never depart.
Let all that you know of Me

Never leave your mind.
Even in uncertainties, I'll always be on time.
Very early every morning, I'll be waiting to talk to you.
Even if tears are your prayers I'll hold you as I always do.
Rid yourself of doubt and

Let faith be your life's way.
Every moment I'll be loving you
And will show you that each day.
Victory is yours My child
Even when you cannot see.

You just trust in My holy Word.
Over and over believe in Me. For
U-are very special and I want you to always know

**That no matter how hard life seems
I'll be with you wherever you go.**

© Dede Toney

Special Recognitions

Barbara Fox

*B*arbara, thank you, for being true to your promise, of editing my book. When I told you I was writing a book you said to me: "when you complete it, I will be glad to edit it." Two years later, your word held true. Thank you for the many hours without pay, that you took to bring my manuscript to life. Thanks for the encouragement and the support you gave me this past year as we worked diligently to bring everything to completion. I truly appreciate your love, time and commitment to me.

Mrs. Fox wrote a review of the book that I would like to share.

With honesty and openness. Dede Dorsey Toney shares her journey that led her into the lap of he Lord. Her story, laced with laughter and tears, offers practical encouragement for daily living.

Her love for people boldly shines through and assures the reader that a relationship with the Lord is the answer. Everyone will be blessed by *Glimpses of God's faithfulness.*

~Barbara Fox- Certified Academic Language Therapist,
Master teacher, friend, encourager, and sister in Christ

Dr. Richard Allen Farmer

D r. Farmer took a look at my book five years ago. He sat down one day and went through the rough draft of the manuscript and gave me wonderful ideas on how to give it wings. He believed in me even when I didn't believe in myself. In fact, when I couldn't quite get things right as the deadline had arrived, I called him and he availed himself to me.

Thank you so much Dr. Farmer. With the Lord's help, I finally did it, just like you said I would do, if I stuck to it. I appreciate all your prayers, your faith in me and your encouragement.

Dr. Farmer also did a review of the book that I would like to share.

Journey with Dede Dorsey Toney as she blends childhood remembrances with practical, biblical advice. Here is an experienced mother and wife, relating to others involved in the challenging privilege of caring for a family. You will profit by this insightful work

~ Dr. Richard Allen Farmer

Financial Supporters

A special thanks goes out to Elizabeth Cannings and Clyde and Jewel Stearns who along with encouragement and prayers, financially supported me in the publishing of this book.

I would like to thank those of you who wanted to give but was not able to give at the time of my asking. I do appreciate all your prayers and encouragement. They meant a lot to me.